FRANCHISING IN KENYA 2014

Legal and Business Considerations

KENDAL H. TYRE, JR., EXECUTIVE EDITOR
DIANA VILMENAY-HAMMOND, MANAGING EDITOR
COURTNEY L. LINDSAY, II, ASSISTANT EDITOR

LEXNOIR FOUNDATION

FIRST QUARTER 2014

LexNoir Foundation is the charitable, educational arm of LexNoir, an international network of lawyers connecting the African Diaspora.

This publication, *Franchising in Kenya 2014: Legal and Business Considerations*, contains excerpts from *Franchising in Africa 2014: Legal and Business Considerations*. Both works are published by LexNoir Foundation and reflect the points of view of the authors and editors as of the date of publication and do not necessarily represent the opinions, interpretations, or positions of the law firms or organizations with which they are affiliated, nor the opinions, interpretations or positions of LexNoir Foundation or LexNoir.

Nothing contained in this book is to be considered as the rendering of legal advice, either generally or in connection with any specific issues or case. Readers are responsible for obtaining advice from their own legal counsel or other professional. This book, any forms and agreements or other information herein are intended for educational and informational purposes only.

www.lexnoir.org

Table of Contents

Franchising in Kenya

John Syekei and Joseph Githaiga
Coulson Harney

i

Bibliography of International Franchise Resources

Kendal H. Tyre, Jr., Diana Vilmenay-Hammond, Pierce Haesung Han, Courtney L. Lindsay, II and Keri McWilliams
Nixon Peabody LLP

Acknowledgment

This book could not have been written without the hard work and dedication of each of the contributing authors and editors. Thank you.

We would like to acknowledge and extend our heartfelt gratitude to Michael Collier and Maria Stallings of the Washington, D.C. office of Nixon Peabody LLP for their invaluable assistance in revising, proofing, and editing this publication.

About the Editors and Authors

Kendal H. Tyre, Jr. – Kendal is a partner in the Washington, D.C. office of Nixon Peabody LLP. He handles domestic and cross-border transactions, including mergers and acquisitions, joint ventures, strategic alliances, licensing, and franchise matters.

In his franchise and licensing practice, Kendal counsels domestic and international franchisors, franchisees, licensors, licensees and distributors regarding U.S. state and federal franchise laws as well as foreign franchise legislation in a variety of jurisdictions. Kendal drafts and provides advice with regard to franchise and license agreements, disclosure documents and area development agreements and has extensive experience drafting and negotiating a variety of other commercial agreements. His client base spans the United States and foreign countries, including South Africa, Kenya, and the United Kingdom.

Kendal is a frequent contributor to franchise publications and a frequent speaker at franchise programs held by the American Bar Association Forum on Franchising and the International Franchise Association.

Kendal is co-chair of the firm's Diversity Action Committee and its Africa Group. Kendal is also the executive director of LexNoir Foundation.

E-mail address: ktyre@nixonpeabody.com

Diana Vilmenay-Hammond – Diana is an attorney in the Washington, D.C. office of Nixon Peabody LLP. She is a member of the firm's Franchise & Distribution Team.

In her franchise practice, Diana works with domestic and international franchisors on transactional and litigation matters. Specifically, she counsels franchisor clients regarding state and federal franchise laws, disclosure and registration obligations.

Diana drafts and negotiates various commercial agreements, including international franchise and development agreements.

Diana has co-authored numerous articles on franchising and frequently co-hosted the Nixon Peabody franchise law webinar series. Topics have included:

- "Franchise Case Law Round-Up: Implications for Your Franchise," February 15, 2012;
- "Social Media Part II: Best Practices in Protecting Your Brand in the New Media," September 14, 2010; and
- "The Awuah Case: Bellwether or Outlier," May 11, 2010

Diana received her J.D. from Howard University School of Law and her B.A. from Georgetown University. She is a member of the American Bar Association (Forum on Franchising).

Email address: dvilmenay@nixonpeabody.com

Pierce Haesung Han – Pierce Haesung Han is an associate in Nixon Peabody's Global Business & Transactions Group. Pierce focuses his practice on three main areas, assisting clients with a variety of complex business transactions.

- Mergers & Acquisitions: Providing assistance to both public and private clients with various mergers and acquisitions, performing due diligence, drafting and negotiating transaction documents, and facilitating closing and post-closing mechanics.
- International Commercial Transactions: Drafting and negotiating a variety of commercial agreements, including international franchise and development agreements, license agreements, and purchase and sale agreements.
- Federal Securities Law Matters: Assisting public and private clients regarding federal securities laws and stock exchange rules relating to corporate governance and disclosure.

Pierce serves as the Secretary of the Asian Pacific Bar Association Educational Fund (an affiliate of the Asian Pacific American Bar Association of the Greater Washington, D.C. Area).

Pierce received his J.D. from Georgetown University Law Center and his B.A. from Case Western Reserve University. He is admitted to practice in the State of New York and the District of Columbia.

E-mail address: phan@nixonpeabody.com

Courtney L. Lindsay II – Courtney L. Lindsay II is an associate in Nixon Peabody's Corporate and Finance practice. In his corporate practice, Courtney assists for-profit and non-profit entities with transactional matters and corporate governance. In various capacities, Courtney has been involved in multiple merger and acquisition transactions, including drafting and managing due diligence.

Previously, Courtney worked in the legal and business affairs department at a national cable network, where he handled matters related to the network's LLC agreement, including drafting board and member consent agreements.

Courtney received his J.D. from the University of Virginia School of Law and his B.A. from the University of Virginia. He is admitted to practice in the Commonwealth of Virginia and the District of Columbia.

E-mail address: clindsay@nixonpeabody.com

Keri McWilliams – Keri is an associate in the Franchise & Distribution team of Nixon Peabody LLP. Keri works with clients on a number of franchising issues, including obtaining and maintaining franchise registrations in various states, responding to state inquiries regarding trade practices, ongoing compliance with state and federal regulations, and updating franchise disclosure documents. She also handles franchise sales counseling and franchise system issues.

Keri is a member of the American Bar Association's Forum on Franchising, and the Federal and Minnesota State bar associations. She is also a member of Minnesota Women Lawyers and the Minnesota Association of Black Lawyers, and a volunteer in the Volunteer Lawyers Network.

Keri received her J.D. from the Georgetown University Law Center and her B.F.A. from Washington University. She is admitted to practice in the District of Columbia and Minnesota.

E-mail address: kmcwilliams@nixonpeabody.com

Joseph Githaiga – Joseph is a senior associate in the Nairobi, Kenya office of Coulson Harney Advocates. He is an accomplished financial services lawyer with more than 14 years post admission experience, including 8 years as an in-house counsel for two of Australia's premier financial institutions – Macquarie Bank Limited and Westpac Banking Corporation. Joseph returned to Kenya in late 2009 to take up a position as a senior lawyer with Coulson Harney. He is a member of the Law Society of New South Wales and the Law Society of Kenya.

During his career in Australia and Kenya, Joseph has advised a broad range of clients including fund managers, insurance companies, banks and private equity investors on a wide variety of commercial legal matters and transactions. Currently, his core practice areas include banking and finance, private equity, regulatory advice and due diligence investigations.

Notable articles that Joseph has published include:

- *"New Business Vehicle in Kenya – Limited Liability Partnerships"* – http://www.coulsonharney.com/News-Blog/Blog/New-Business-Vehicle-in-Kenya-Limited-Liability-Partnerships

- *"Intellectual Property Law and the Protection of Indigenous Folklore & Knowledge"*, E-Law - Murdoch University Electronic Journal of Law, V5 No.2, June 1998

E-mail address: j.githaiga@coulsonharney.com

John Syekei – John Syekei is a partner in the Nairobi, Kenya office of Coulson Harney Advocates. He was admitted as an Advocate in 2005. He trained at Daly & Figgis Advocates and Deloitte and headed the Intellectual Property Department at a leading firm as a partner until joining Coulson Harney in March 2010. He was admitted into the Coulson Harney partnership on March 1, 2011.

John advises clients on M&A transactions in the IT, telecommunications and healthcare sectors. His practice areas and experience cover commercial intellectual property advice, IP litigation, advertising law and litigation, advice on drafting and/or negotiation of information technology agreements on the seller or buyer side, and advice on the protection and enforcement of trade mark, patent, copyright and industrial designs. He practices across Africa directly for local clients. He also acts for clients in intellectual property infringement actions, anti-counterfeiting raids, due diligence investigations and reports, drafting of licensing and franchise agreements, trade mark oppositions, trade mark cancellations and domain name dispute resolutions before WIPO.

E-mail address: j.syekei@coulsonharney.com

About the Book

Franchising in Kenya 2014: Legal and Business Considerations contains excerpts from the larger work, *Franchising in Africa 2014: Legal and Business Considerations.* Both books serve as practical, succinct, easy-to-use reference tools for lawyers, business people and academics to use in navigating the myriad laws and business issues impacting franchise arrangements on the African continent.

This book provides an overview of the franchise industry in Kenya and addresses the typical legal issues confronted when expanding a franchise system in Kenya. The larger work, *Franchising in Africa 2014: Legal and Business Considerations*, covers those laws governing franchising in fifteen other African countries – Angola, Botswana, Burundi, Cape Verde, Democratic Republic of Congo, Egypt, Ethiopia, Ghana, Mozambique, Nigeria, Rwanda, South Africa, Tunisia, Zambia and Zimbabwe.

In both books, an author, who is a legal expert in the designated jurisdiction, addresses the basic questions that a franchise lawyer would need to know to competently represent a client in expanding their franchise system to that country.

Each country chapter organizes a discussion of that country's laws under various headings and in a uniform format. Topics were sent to each country's author in the form of a questionnaire, and each author drafted responses to the questions presented. A general overview relating to the political and economic history of the country at the beginning of each chapter provides an initial context for the regulatory framework.[1]

---

[1] The source of information for these sections is the Central Intelligence Agency, https://www.cia.gov/library/publications/the-world-factbook/ (last visited November 3, 2013).

Apart from an overview of the legal framework for franchising, each book contains other articles and resources that should prove useful to those in the franchise industry.

The authors for each chapter are listed at the beginning of a chapter and their biographical information is listed in the previous section, *About the Editors and Authors*.

Readers should always consult with local counsel in the relevant jurisdiction instead of relying solely on the information contained in this book. The laws governing franchising are evolving and local counsel in Kenya are best positioned to provide timely, relevant advice applying the current law to the particular facts of a case.

Franchising in Kenya

John Syekei and Joseph Githaiga

Coulson Harney

Nairobi, Kenya

Kenya

I.   Introduction

A.   Historical Background of Country

Founding president Jomo Kenyatta led Kenya from independence in 1963 until his death in 1978, when President Daniel Toroitich arap Moi took power in constitutional succession. Kenya was a de facto one-party state from 1969 until 1982. Close to 30 years later, in August 2010, Kenyans overwhelmingly adopted a new constitution in a national referendum. The new constitution introduced additional checks and balances to executive power and significant devolution of power and resources to 47 newly created counties. The first presidential election under the new constitution occurred on March 4, 2013. Uhuru Kenyatta, the son of founding president Jomo Kenyatta, won the March elections in the first round by a close margin and was sworn into office on April 9, 2013.

B.   Economy of the Country

Kenya is the leading economy in East Africa and the hub for a majority of the foreign investment into the region. The growth of Kenya's economy has traditionally been underpinned by the tourism and agricultural industries (primarily exports of tea, coffee and horticultural produce). However, over the last decade there has been a sustained government effort to diversify the economy, which, combined with investments from an active and engaged private sector, have resulted in remarkable developments in areas such as the telecommunications and IT sectors and the banking and insurance services industries. In addition, heavy annual remittances from the Kenyan diaspora have helped to further spur economic growth. Kenya now boasts some of the fastest growing urban centres on the continent, with Nairobi, the capital, being a showcase for this phenomenon – with its new malls, new roads, new hotels and new gated communities. Recent discoveries in oil and gas as well as rare minerals are set to further boost the Kenyan growth story and cement its position as the regional powerhouse in East Africa. To effectively do so though, Kenya will also have to tackle key

1

Kenya

economic challenges such as high youth unemployment, spiraling budget deficits, inflationary pressures and exchange rate fluctuations.

C.   Franchise Legal Overview

There are no specific laws in Kenya governing franchise agreements. Franchise agreements are generally regulated by the law of contract as applicable in Kenya.[2]

II.   Regulatory Requirements

A.   Pre-Sale Disclosure

Please describe any pre-sale franchise disclosure or similar requirements that may apply to franchise transactions.

---

[2]   There are two sources of laws in Kenya – statutory law and non-statutory law. Kenyan statutory law is contained in statutes that were adopted from British colonial times and statutes which have been passed since December 12, 1963 (the date of independence). The pre-independence acts that were adopted subsequent to the date of independence are very similar to if not identical to acts dealing with similar subjects in other former British colonies such as Uganda, Tanzania, Zambia, Malawi and Zimbabwe. The post-independence acts are largely derived from English acts on similar subjects with appropriate modifications for local circumstances. The adoption of a new Constitution for Kenya in August 2010 has brought, and will continue to bring, significant changes to the political, judicial and administrative systems of Kenya. It also requires a large number of new laws to be enacted, either to replace current statutes, or to legislate for new aspects. This is likely to take several years to complete, notwithstanding that the process has begun.

Most of the non-statutory law in Kenya is based on English common law and equitable principles but in addition, a section of common law has also developed from decisions of the Kenyan courts since the date of independence. Much of this latter section of law is based on the decisions of English courts and the courts of other countries in the commonwealth. Kenyan courts are not bound by these decisions, but they regard them to be highly persuasive if similar facts and law are involved and they are clearly not repugnant to the interests and circumstances of Kenya and its inhabitants. Consequently, most of the commercial law which is not specifically covered by Kenyan statutes is based on English common law.

Kenya

Kenyan law does not prescribe any pre-sale disclosure requirements to franchise transactions.

B. Governmental Approvals, Registrations, Filing Requirements

Please describe any necessary government approvals, registrations, or filing requirements that may apply to franchise transactions.

There are no specific approval, registration or filing requirements for franchise agreements. Nonetheless, particular franchise agreements or arrangements may fall within the ambit of the *Competition Act, 2010* ("Act") if they are determined to be restrictive trade practices, that is,

> *"agreements between undertakings, decisions by associations of undertakings, decisions by undertakings or concerted practices by undertakings which have as their object or effect the prevention, distortion or lessening of competition in trade in goods or services in Kenya, or a part of Kenya".*

Examples of restricted practices under the Act include:

a) directly or indirectly fixing purchase or sales prices or any other trading conditions;

b) dividing markets by allocating customers, suppliers, areas or specific types of goods or services;

c) involving a practice of minimum resale price maintenance;

d) limiting or controlling production, market outlets or access, technical development or investment; or

e) otherwise preventing, distorting or restricting competition.

The foregoing practices are prohibited unless they have been specifically exempted under the Act by the Competition

Kenya

Authority ("Authority"). The application for exemption must be in the prescribed manner and accompanied by such information as may be prescribed or as the Authority may reasonably require.

The Authority in determining the application for exemption may:

a) grant the exemption;

b) refuse to grant the exemption, and notify the applicant accordingly with a statement of the reasons for the refusal; or

c) issue a certificate of clearance stating that in its opinion, on the basis of the facts in its possession, the agreement, decision or concerted practice or the category of agreements, decisions or concerted practices does not constitute a restricted trade practice.

The nature of the franchise business may also require the franchisor to seek a license if it operates or proposes to operate in a regulated industry, for example, telecommunications, insurance, banking and so on.

C.   Limits of Fees and Typical Term of Franchise Agreement

Please describe any limits upon the nature and extent of fees and the term of a typical franchise agreement.

There are no term limits that apply specifically to franchise agreements and, generally, the parties to the agreement are free to agree on the nature and extent of fees.

III.   Currency

If all payments under a franchise agreement must be made in immediately available U.S. Dollars, please advise as to any restrictions, reporting requirements, or regulations concerning the exchange, repatriation, or remittance of U.S. Dollars.

Kenya

There are currently no exchange controls applicable in Kenya that restrict the repatriation or remittance of foreign currency.

The *Central Bank Act, Cap 491 of the Laws of Kenya*[3], states that, except with the permission of the Central Bank, the following transactions must be effected through an authorized bank:

a) payments in Kenya, to or for the credit of a person outside Kenya;

b) payments outside Kenya, to or for the credit of a person in Kenya; or

c) payments in Kenya (other than a payment for a current transaction[4]) between a resident and non-resident.

Accordingly, under the Central Bank Act, a person may seek the permission of the Central Bank of Kenya to exempt one of the types of transactions listed above from transfer through an authorized bank. A person who contravenes the above provisions commits an offence and shall be liable on conviction to a fine not exceeding five hundred thousand shillings (approximately US$5,786) or to imprisonment for a term not exceeding three years, or to both.

IV. Taxes, Tariffs, and Duties

Please do not provide any in-depth comments on tax structuring. However, please provide your general comments on the typical amount of withholding tax that would apply and whether a

---

[3] Section 33H of the Central Bank Act.

[4] According to Section 2 of the Central Bank Act, a "payment for a current transaction" is a payment other than a payment for transferring capital. It includes: (1) a payment due in connection with trade; (2) a payment due as interest or as net income or return from other investment; (3) a payment for amortization of a loan or for depreciation of direct investment; or (4) a remittance for family living expenses.

Kenya

"gross-up" provision contained in a franchise agreement would be enforceable in your country.

In Kenya, withholding tax is applicable to dividends, interest, royalties and technical services fees.

With regard to dividends, no withholding tax is imposed if the recipient is a qualifying Kenyan financial institution or the resident recipient company controls 12.5% or more of the capital of the payer. Otherwise, the rate is 5% for dividends paid to residents of Kenya and on listed shares for citizens of the East African Community. A rate of 10% applies for other nonresidents.

With regard to interest, there are different categories for withholding tax on interest. Interest received from financial institutions is subject to a 15% tax, while the withholding tax on interest on bearer certificates is 25%. Withholding tax on interest from bearer bonds is 10%.

Royalties paid to a resident are subject to a 5% withholding tax whereas the rate of 20% applies if royalties are paid to a nonresident.

A withholding tax of 10% is levied on the payment of technical service fees (as well as professional/management fees) where the services are provided by a resident. The rate is 20% where the service provider is nonresident.

Kenya is a party to double taxation treaties with a number of countries including Zambia, Norway, Denmark, Sweden, the United Kingdom, Germany, Canada and India. Kenya has also signed double taxation treaties with Italy, Tanzania and Uganda but they are not in force as they have not been ratified.

Gross-up provisions are recognized under Kenyan law and are common in agreements entered into in Kenya.

Kenya

V.   Trademarks

Please advise us as to whether there are any special requirements for granting a valid trademark license, including the use of a registered user agreement or a short trademark license agreement and any required filing of such an agreement with the trademark authorities.

Any trademarks that are the subject of a franchise agreement need to be registered. The registration of trademarks in Kenya is similar to the procedure in most common law jurisdictions.

The *Trade Marks Act, Cap 506 of the Laws of Kenya* ("TMA"), allows for a person other than the proprietor of a trademark to be registered as a licensee thereof.

For a person to be registered as a licensee of a trademark, the proprietor and the proposed licensee are required to apply in writing to the Registrar of Trade Marks in the prescribed manner and furnish him or her with a statutory declaration made by the proprietor, or by some person authorized to act on his or her behalf and approved by the Registrar stating:

a)   particulars of the relationship, existing or proposed, between the proprietor and the proposed licensee, including particulars showing the degree of control by the proprietor over the permitted use which their relationship will confer and whether it is a term of their relationship that the proposed licensee shall be the sole licensee or that there shall be any other restriction as to persons for whose registration as licensees application may be made;

b)   the goods or services in respect of which registration is proposed;

c)   any conditions or restrictions proposed with respect to the characteristics of the goods or services, to the mode or place of permitted use or to any other matter; and

d) whether the permitted use is to be for a period or without limit of period, and if for a period the duration thereof.

The Registrar should also be provided with such further documents, information or evidence as he or she may be require or as may be required under rules made pursuant to the TMA.

The TMA allows the Registrar to refuse registration as described above if it appears to him or her that such a grant would tend to facilitate trafficking in a trade mark.

The TMA does not prescribe the time it would take for the registration of a license with respect to a trademark. However, based on our experience we estimate that the registration process would approximately take 2 months.

VI. Restrictions on Transfer

Please advise as to whether there are any restrictions (1) on a franchisor to restrict transfers by a master franchisee, any interest in a master franchisee, or the assets of the master franchisee or (2) the ability of a master franchisee to control and/or restrict transfers of a subfranchisee's rights under a master franchise agreement, interest in the subfranchisee, or the assets of the subfranchisee.

Since there is no specific law in Kenya governing franchise arrangements, the provisions applicable to a franchise arrangement are dependent on the agreement reached between the franchisor and the franchisee and are therefore governed by the *Law of Contract Act, Cap 23 of the Laws of Kenya*, and the common law principles on contract.

Parties to a franchise agreement are free to incorporate transfer restrictions into the franchise agreement.

The inclusion of such restrictions in a particular franchise agreement and their enforceability may nonetheless be affected by other agreements entered into by a party to the franchise agreement with a third party. Such third party agreements may prohibit the exercise of the restrictions in the franchise agreement without the consent of the third party (for example a third party agreement with a bank may prohibit an assignment of the franchise agreement or the transfer of the franchise business without the prior written consent of the bank).

VII. Termination

Please advise us as to any laws relating to termination in your country, such as agency laws, required indemnity provisions, notice or "good cause" requirements, or other laws affecting termination of a franchise agreement. Please describe.

Generally, the termination of a contract is a matter typically governed by the contract between the parties and is not prescribed in statute. English common law principles on agency and contract apply in Kenya in construing such provisions in a contract.

VIII. Governing Law, Jurisdiction, and Dispute Resolution

A.   Choice of Law of Foreign Jurisdiction

Please confirm whether the choice of law of a foreign jurisdiction would likely to be upheld under the law of the country, except for certain matters such as trademarks, bankruptcy, and competition matters, which we assume would be governed by the law in your country.

Kenyan courts generally observe choice of law and forum clauses. A contract is governed by the law chosen by the parties. The choice can be expressed or demonstrated with reasonable certainty by the terms of the contract. Kenyan courts will disregard the application of a rule of foreign law where it application would be contrary to public policy.

Kenya

B.   International Arbitration Dispute Resolution

Please confirm that a court in your country would honor an election of international arbitration dispute resolution, and therefore refuse to hear any disputes arising under a franchise agreement.

Kenyan Courts would honor and uphold an election of international dispute resolution, if the parties have by agreement agreed to such submission. Therefore, if a franchise agreement provides that a dispute is to be submitted to arbitration in a foreign country, Kenyan courts will refuse to entertain a claim and would direct the parties to resolve the dispute through arbitration as provided for in the franchise agreement.

Kenya is a signatory to the 1958 New York Convention on the Recognition and Enforcement of Foreign Arbitral Awards (the "New York Convention"). The Arbitration Act provides that an international arbitration award shall be recognized as binding and enforced in accordance with the provisions of the New York Convention or any other convention to which Kenya is signatory and relating to arbitral awards.

IX.   Non-Competition Provisions

If the franchise agreement prohibits the master franchisee from engaging in certain competitive activities during the term of the agreement, and for a 12-month period after the termination or expiration of the agreement, please comment on the enforceability of non-competition covenants in your country.

Non-competition covenants in Kenya are governed by the *Contracts in Restraint of Trade Act, Cap 24 of the Laws of Kenya* ("CRTA"). Such covenants may be included in contracts but the court may strike them out where a party to an agreement challenging the clause proves that they are unreasonable.

Kenya

The CRTA specifically provides that any agreement or contract that contains a provision or covenant whereby a party to the agreement is restrained from exercising any lawful profession, trade, business or occupation shall not be void only on the ground that the provision or covenant is contained in the agreement. However, the High Court shall have power to declare the provision or covenant to be void where the court is satisfied that, having regard to the nature of the profession, trade, business or occupation concerned, and the period of time and the area within which it is expressed to apply, and to all the circumstances of the case, the provision or covenant is not reasonable either:

- in the interests of the parties, (in that it affords more than adequate protection to the party in whose favor it is imposed); or

- in the interests of the public (in that it is not injurious to the public interest).

X.   Language Requirements

Does the law in your country require that a franchise agreement be translated into the local language in order to be enforceable between the parties?

There is no specific provision in Kenyan law requiring that a franchise agreement be translated for it to be enforceable between the parties.

XI.   Other Significant Matters

Please advise as to whether there are any significant matters not addressed above of which a franchisor should be aware in connection with its entering into a franchise agreement in your country.

Since there is no specific legislation governing franchise agreements in Kenya, there are no comprehensive legal

Kenya

requirements applicable to franchise agreements other than the ones discussed herein.

There is no franchise association in Kenya which may be as a result of the fact that franchise arrangements involving Kenyan entities are not common and are mainly used by multinational brands. Examples of franchise brands in Kenya include the Hilton Hotel, Intercontinental Hotel, Crown Plaza and Kentucky Fried Chicken (KFC).

Bibliography of International Franchise Resources

Kendal H. Tyre, Jr., Diana Vilmenay-Hammond, Pierce Haesung Han, Courtney L. Lindsay II and Keri McWilliams

Nixon Peabody LLP

Washington, D.C.

I. General International Resources

Mark Abell, Gary R. Duvall, and Andrea Oricchio Kirsh, *International Franchise Legislation* B1, ABA FORUM ON FRANCHISING (1996)

Kathleen C. Anderson and Anthony M. Stiegler, *Put Muscle in Your Marks: Enforcing Intellectual Property Rights* W14, ABA FORUM ON FRANCHISING (1995)

Richard M. Asbill and Jane W. LaFranchi, *International Franchise Sales Laws—A Survey* W7, ABA FORUM ON FRANCHISING (2005)

Jeffery A. Brimer, Alison C. McElroy, and John Pratt, *Going International: What Additional Restraints Will You Face?* W4, ABA FORUM ON FRANCHISING (2011)

Michael G. Brennan, Alexander Konigsberg, and Philip F. Zeidman, *Globetrotting: A Workshop on International Franchising* 10/W8, ABA FORUM ON FRANCHISING (1994)

Michael G. Brennan, Alexander Konigsberg, and Philip F. Zeidman, *Globetrotting: Strategies for Launching U.S. Franchisors Abroad* 2/P2, ABA FORUM ON FRANCHISING (1994)

Christopher P. Bussert and Jennifer Dolman, *Regaining Your Trademark After Abandonment or Misappropriation* W7, ABA FORUM ON FRANCHISING (2011)

Ronald T. Coleman and Linda K. Stevens, *Trade Secrets and Confidential Information: Rights and Remedies* W2, ABA FORUM ON FRANCHISING (2000)

Finola Cunningham, *Commerce Department Helps Franchisors Go Global*, in FRANCHISING WORLD 63 (Dec. 2005)

Michael R. Daigle and Alex S. Konigsberg, *Meeting Off-Shore Disclosure and Contract Requirements* F/W13, ABA FORUM ON FRANCHISING (1992)

Jennifer Dolman, Robert A. Lauer, and Lawrence M. Weinberg, *Structuring International Master Franchise Relationships for Success and Responding When Things Go Awry* W22, ABA FORUM ON FRANCHISING (2007)

Gary R. Duvall, Paul Jones, and Jane LaFranchi, *Planning for the International Enforcement of Franchise Agreements* W6, ABA FORUM ON FRANCHISING (1999)

William Edwards, *International Expansion: Do Opportunities Outweigh Challenges?* in FRANCHISING WORLD (February 2008)

George J. Eydt and Stuart Hershman, *Bringing a Foreign Franchise System to the United States* W9, ABA FORUM ON FRANCHISING (2009)

William A. Finkelstein and Louis T. Pirkey, *International Trademarks* W15, ABA FORUM ON FRANCHISING (1991)

William A. Finkelstein, *Protecting Trademarks Internationally: Current Strategies and Developments* B3, ABA FORUM ON FRANCHISING (1996)

Stephen Giles, Lou H. Jones, and Lawrence Weinberg, *Negotiating and Documenting Complex International Franchise Agreements* W21, ABA FORUM ON FRANCHISING (2006)

Steven M. Goldman, Stephen Giles, Marc Israel, and Stanley Wong, *Competition Round Up from Around the World* LB2, ABA FORUM ON FRANCHISING (2004)

David C. Gryce and E. Lynn Perry, *Trademarks and Copyrights in the International Arena* 6/W4, ABA FORUM ON FRANCHISING (1993)

Kenneth S. Kaplan, Andrew P. Loewinger, and Penelope J. Ward, *System Standards in International Franchising* W14, ABA FORUM ON FRANCHISING (2005)

Edward Levitt and Jorge Mondragon, *A Survey of International Legal Traps and How to Avoid Them—Beyond the Franchise Laws* W20, ABA FORUM ON FRANCHISING (2007)

Ned Levitt, Kendal H. Tyre, and Penny Ward, *The Impossible Dream: Controlling Your International Franchise System* W4, ABA FORUM ON FRANCHISING (2010)

Michael K. Lindsey and Andrew P. Loewinger, *International (Non-U.S.) Franchise Disclosure Requirements* W9, ABA FORUM ON FRANCHISING (2002)

Andrew P. Loewinger and John Pratt, *Recent Changes and Trends in International Franchise Laws* W4, ABA FORUM ON FRANCHISING (2008)

Andrew P. Loewinger and Thomas M. Pitegoff, *Avoiding the Long Arm of the Law in International Franchising: Issues and Approaches* W8, ABA FORUM ON FRANCHISING (1995)

Craig J. Madson and Katherine C. Spelman, *Similarity and Confusion in the Intellectual Property Arena* W11, ABA FORUM ON FRANCHISING (1997)

Christopher A. Nowak, John Pratt, and Carl E. Zwisler, *Franchising Internationally with Countries with Opaque Legal Systems* W20, ABA FORUM ON FRANCHISING (2006)

E. Lynn Perry and John L. Sullivan Jr., *Trademark Compliance and Enforcement Techniques* E/W12, ABA FORUM ON FRANCHISING (1992)

Marcel Portmann, *Franchising Sector Proves Global Reach*, in FRANCHISING WORLD (January 2007)

John Pratt and Luiz Henrique O. do Amaral, *Civil Law for Common Law Practitioners (or How to Draft an Agreement for Use Overseas)* W4, ABA FORUM ON FRANCHISING (2002)

Kirk W. Reilly, Robert F. Salkowski and Geoffrey B. Shaw, *Determining the Rules of Engagement in Litigation Here and Abroad* W5, ABA FORUM ON FRANCHISING (2008)

Catherine Riesterer and Frank Zaid, *Basics of International Franchising* L/B2, ABA FORUM ON FRANCHISING (1997)

W. Andrew Scott and Christopher N. Wormald, *Stranger in a Strange Land: Contrasting Franchising in International Expansion* W2, ABA FORUM ON FRANCHISING (2003)

Donald Smith and Erik Wulff, *International Franchising: The Unraveling of an International Franchise Relationship* 15/W13, ABA FORUM ON FRANCHISING (1993)

Frank Zaid, Pamela Mills, and Michael Santa Maria, *Essential Issues in International Franchising* LB/1, ABA FORUM ON FRANCHISING (2001)

II.   African Resources

Joyce G. Mazero and J. Perry Maisonneuve, *Franchising in the Middle East and North Africa* W2, ABA FORUM ON FRANCHISING (2009)

Kendal H. Tyre, Jr. and Diana Vilmenay-Hammond, *Franchise World: A Burgeoning Middle Class Spurs Franchise Investment in Africa*, MINORITY BUSINESS ENTREPRENEUR (November 2012)

Kendal H. Tyre, Jr., *IP Protection May Promote Additional Franchise Growth in Africa*, NIXON PEABODY LLP: FRANCHISING BUSINESS & LAW ALERT (September 2012)

Kendal H. Tyre, Jr., *Market Potential for Franchising in Africa*, NIXON PEABODY LLP: FRANCHISING BUSINESS & LAW ALERT (June 2011)

Kendal H. Tyre, Jr. and Courtney L. Lindsay, II, *Continued Growth of Franchising in Africa*, NIXON PEABODY LLP: FRANCHISE LAW ALERT (April 2013)

Kendal H. Tyre, Jr. and Courtney L. Lindsay, II, *Pan African Franchise Federation Holds Inaugural Meeting*, NIXON PEABODY LLP: AFRICA ALERT (June 2013)

Kendal H. Tyre, Jr. and Courtney L. Lindsay, II, *White House Encouraging Private Investment and Transparency in Sub-Saharan Africa*, NIXON PEABODY LLP: AFRICA ALERT (August 2012)

Kendal H. Tyre, Jr. and Diana Vilmenay-Hammond, *African Economic Growth Impacts Franchising on the Continent*, NIXON PEABODY LLP: FRANCHISE LAW ALERT (July 2012)

Kendal H. Tyre, Jr. and Diana Vilmenay-Hammond, *Franchising in Africa*, in FRANCHISING WORLD (August 2013)

John Sotos and Sam Hall, *African Franchising: Cross-Continent Momentum*, in FRANCHISING WORLD (June 2007)

A. Angola

João Afonso Fialho, *Franchising in Angola*, in FRANCHISING IN AFRICA: LEGAL AND BUSINESS CONSIDERATIONS 91-105 (Kendal H. Tyre, Jr. & Diana Vilmenay-Hammond eds. 2012)

B.   Botswana

Bonzo Makgalemele, *Franchising in Botswana*, in FRANCHISING
IN AFRICA: LEGAL AND BUSINESS CONSIDERATIONS 107-117
(Kendal H. Tyre, Jr. & Diana Vilmenay-Hammond eds. 2012)

C.   Cape Verde

João Afonso Fialho, *Franchising in Cape Verde*, in
FRANCHISING IN AFRICA: LEGAL AND BUSINESS
CONSIDERATIONS 119-132 (Kendal H. Tyre, Jr. & Diana
Vilmenay-Hammond eds. 2012)

D.   Egypt

Girgis Abd El-Shahid, *Franchising in Eqypt*, in FRANCHISING IN
AFRICA: LEGAL AND BUSINESS CONSIDERATIONS 133-142
(Kendal H. Tyre, Jr. & Diana Vilmenay-Hammond eds. 2012)

A. Safaa El Din El Oteifi, *Egypt*, in INTERNATIONAL
FRANCHISING EGY/1 (Dennis Campbell gen. ed. 2011)

E.   Ethiopia

Yohannes Assefa and Biset Beyene Molla, *Franchising in
Ethiopia*, in FRANCHISING IN AFRICA: LEGAL AND BUSINESS
CONSIDERATIONS 143-157 (Kendal H. Tyre, Jr. & Diana
Vilmenay-Hammond eds. 2012)

Kendal H. Tyre, Jr., Yohannes Assefa and Getachew Mengistie
Alemu, *New Intellectual Property Regulation Requires Scramble
to Protect Marks in Ethiopia*, NIXON PEABODY LLP: AFRICA
ALERT (October 2013)

F.   Ghana

Divine K.D. Letsa and Hawa Tejansie Ajei, *Franchising in
Ghana*, in FRANCHISING IN AFRICA: LEGAL AND BUSINESS
CONSIDERATIONS 159-167 (Kendal H. Tyre, Jr. & Diana
Vilmenay-Hammond eds. 2012)

G. Libya

Kendal H. Tyre, Jr. & Diana Vilmenay-Hammond, *First U.S. Franchise Opens in Libya*, NIXON PEABODY LLP: AFRICA ALERT (August 2012)

H. Mozambique

Diogo Xavier da Cunha, *Franchising in Mozambique*, in FRANCHISING IN AFRICA: LEGAL AND BUSINESS CONSIDERATIONS 169-182 (Kendal H. Tyre, Jr. & Diana Vilmenay-Hammond eds. 2012)

I. Nigeria

Theo Emuwa and Bimbola Fowler-Ekar, *Franchising in Nigeria*, in FRANCHISING IN AFRICA: LEGAL AND BUSINESS CONSIDERATIONS 183-198 (Kendal H. Tyre, Jr. & Diana Vilmenay-Hammond eds. 2012)

Kendal H. Tyre, Jr. and Theo Emuwa, *Nigerian Franchising: Making Your Way Through the Thicket*, NIXON PEABODY LLP: FRANCHISE LAW ALERT (June 2005)

J. South Africa

Eugene Honey, *Franchising and the New Consumer Protection Bill*, BOWMAN GILFILLAN (March 2008)

Eugene Honey, *Franchising and the Consumer Protection Bill*, BOWMAN GILFILLAN (May 2008)

Eugene Honey, *Pitfalls and Difficulties with the CPA*, ADAMS & ADAMS (March 2013)

Eugene Honey, *Disclosure is Compulsory*, ADAMS & ADAMS (May 2013)

Eugene Honey and Wim Alberts, *Fundamental Consumer Rights: The Right to Equality*, BOWMAN GILFILLAN (March 2009)

Eugene Honey and Wim Alberts, *The Reach of the Consumer Protection Bill: The Final*, BOWMAN GILFILLAN (March 2009)

Eugene Honey, *South Africa*, in GETTING THE DEAL THROUGH: FRANCHISE (2013) 172-178 (Philip F. Zeidman ed. 2013)

Taswell Papier, *Franchising in South Africa*, in FRANCHISING IN AFRICA: LEGAL AND BUSINESS CONSIDERATIONS 199-224 (Kendal H. Tyre, Jr. & Diana Vilmenay-Hammond eds. 2012)

Kendal H. Tyre, Jr., *A New Legal Landscape for Franchising in South Africa*, NIXON PEABODY LLP: FRANCHISING BUSINESS & LAW ALERT (September 2009)

K.   Tunisia

Yessine Ferah, *Franchising in Tunisia*, in FRANCHISING IN AFRICA: LEGAL AND BUSINESS CONSIDERATIONS 225-245 (Kendal H. Tyre, Jr. & Diana Vilmenay-Hammond eds. 2012)

Kendal H. Tyre, Jr., Diana Vilmenay-Hammond, and Yessine Ferah, *New Franchise Legislation in Tunisia*, NIXON PEABODY LLP: FRANCHISE LAW ALERT (September 2010)

L.   Zambia

Mabvuto Sakala, *Franchising in Zambia*, in FRANCHISING IN AFRICA: LEGAL AND BUSINESS CONSIDERATIONS 247-255 (Kendal H. Tyre, Jr. & Diana Vilmenay-Hammond eds. 2012)

14730046.1

www.ingramcontent.com/pod-product-compliance
Lightning Source LLC
Chambersburg PA
CBHW060325220326
41598CB00027B/4426